the StepStoolChef®
Cookbook for Kids

Where Kids Are The Chefs, Parents Are The Assistants

© 2016 The Step Stool Chef® All Rights Reserved.

The Step Stool Chef® name and logo are trademarks registered in the U.S. Patent and Trademark Office.
Photo Credit (cover, back cover, Table of Contents): Creative Soul Photography
ISBN-978-1-365-03254-7

About this Cookbook

Kids are always being asked to be a "helper" in the kitchen. Well now, here's their chance to be the chef in the kitchen while the adults be the assistant.

Kid cooking is a perfect way to **boost self-esteem** and **build confidence** while learning new skills that will last a lifetime.

The **Step Stool Chef**® is sharing some of his favorite recipes that are easy and fun for kids to cook. We have included **step-by-step photos** of each recipe in the back of the cookbook to show how kids can do it themselves.

To get started, here are

3 Simple Rules to Kid Cooking

Know Your ABC's

Always Be Cooking
It's ok to make mistakes, but it's not ok to give up

Always Be Careful
Practice good listening skills and pay careful attention

Always Be Cleaning
Clean as you go to prevent a big mess

Oh and remember **Kids Lead, Parents Assist!**

Have Fun and Happy Cooking!

Table of Contents

- **4** Baked Apple Pie Bites
- **6** Dutch Apple Crisp
- **8** Easy Peesy Cheesy Puffs
- **10** Mini-Muffin Chicken Pot Pie
- **12** Pizza Burgers
- **14** Salmon with Brown Sugar Glaze
- **16** Sausage Bites with Maple Lemon Sauce
- **18** Strawberry Salsa with Cinnamon Pita Chips
- **20** Taco Buddies
- **22** Turkey Sausage Popovers
- **24-34** Step-by-Step Guide for Each Recipe

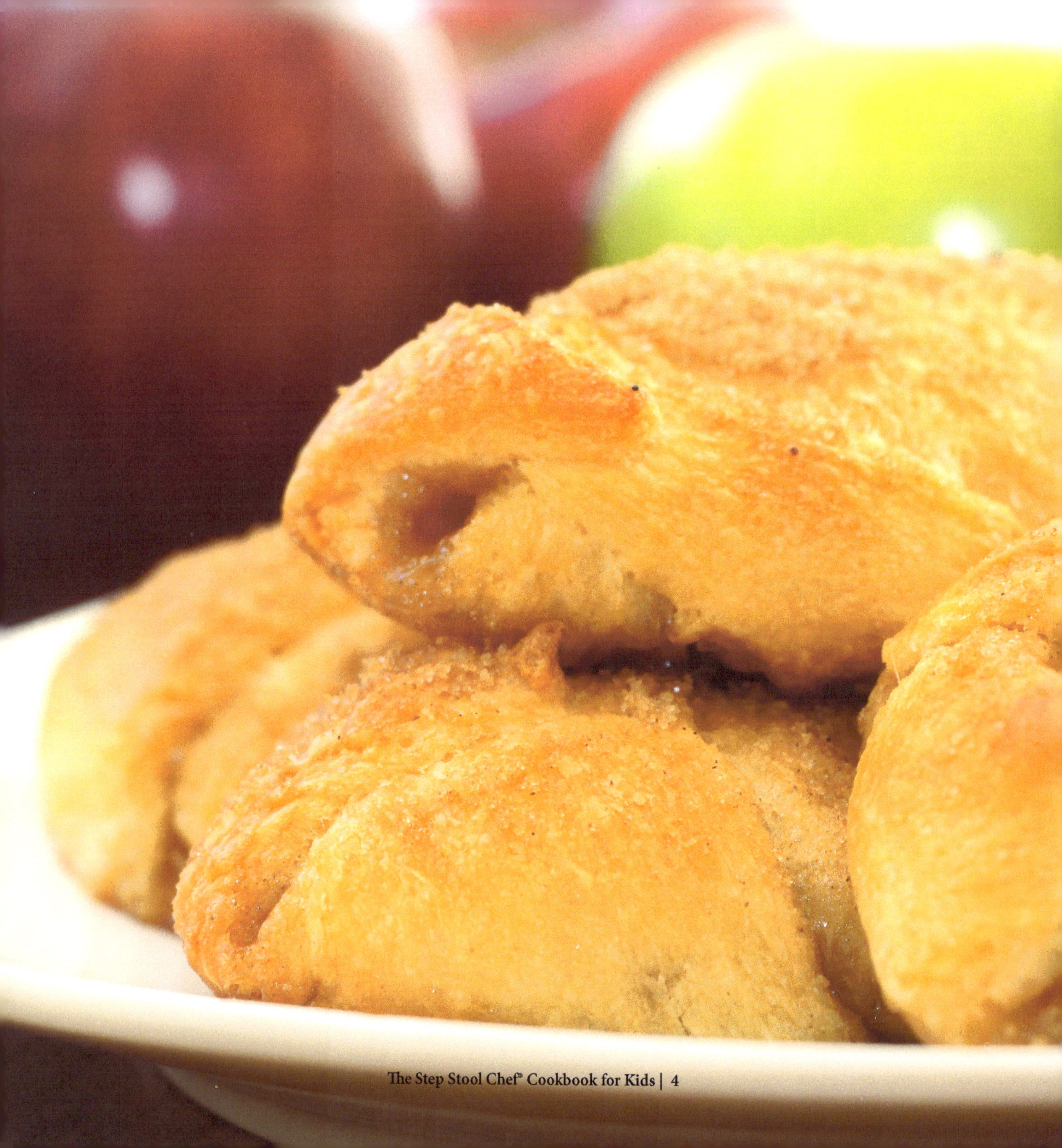

today's special

Baked Apple Bites

INGREDIENTS

1 apple, peeled and cut into 8 slices
2 tablespoons butter, melted
1 can refrigerated crescent roll dough

1/3 cup brown sugar
1 teaspoon cinnamon
1 teaspoon nutmeg

INSTRUCTIONS

1. Preheat oven to 375 degrees.
2. Peel apple then cut into 8 slices around the core. Using an apple slicer will make this easier.
3. Pour 1 tablespoon of melted butter over the apple slices in a bowl.
4. In a separate small bowl, mix the brown sugar, cinnamon and nutmeg.
5. Unroll the crescent dough and separate into 8 triangles on a baking sheet lined with parchment paper.
6. Sprinkle sugar mixture evenly among triangles then place an apple slice at the wide end of the triangle.
7. Starting at the wide end of each triangle, roll the apple in the crescent dough. Brush the top with remaining tablespoon of melted butter then sprinkle the top with remaining sugar mixture.
8. Bake for 10-15 minutes then let cool for 5 minutes. Then enjoy!

Step-by-Step Recipe on page 24

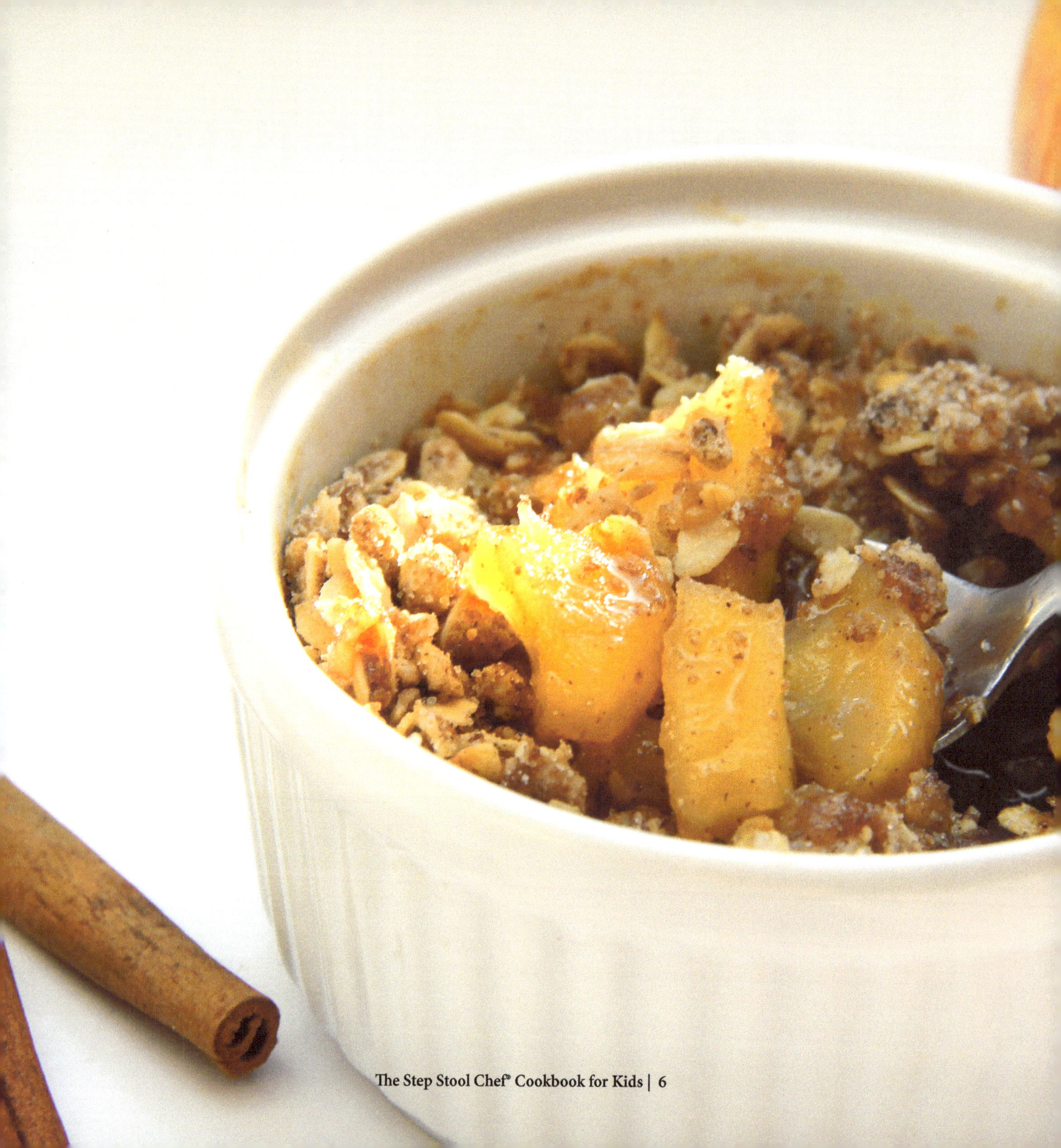

today's special

Dutch Apple Crisp

INGREDIENTS

FOR FILLING
5 apples, peeled, cored, and diced
1/2 cup honey
1 lemon, juiced 1 teaspoon vanilla extract
1 teaspoon cinnamon
1/4 teaspoon nutmeg

FOR TOPPING
1 cup oats
1/2 cup flour
1/4 cup brown sugar
1/4 cup butter
1/2 teaspoon cinnamon

Step-by-Step Recipe on page 25

INSTRUCTIONS

1. Preheat oven to 375 degrees.
2. Lightly grease ramekin cups or baking dish with cooking spray.
3. Combine the ingredients for the filling in a mixing bowl then set aside.
4. Combine the ingredients for the topping in a separate mixing bowl.
5. Place apples in a ramekin cup or baking dish then sprinkle topping over apple.
6. Bake for 30-40 minutes in preheated oven. Let cool & serve!

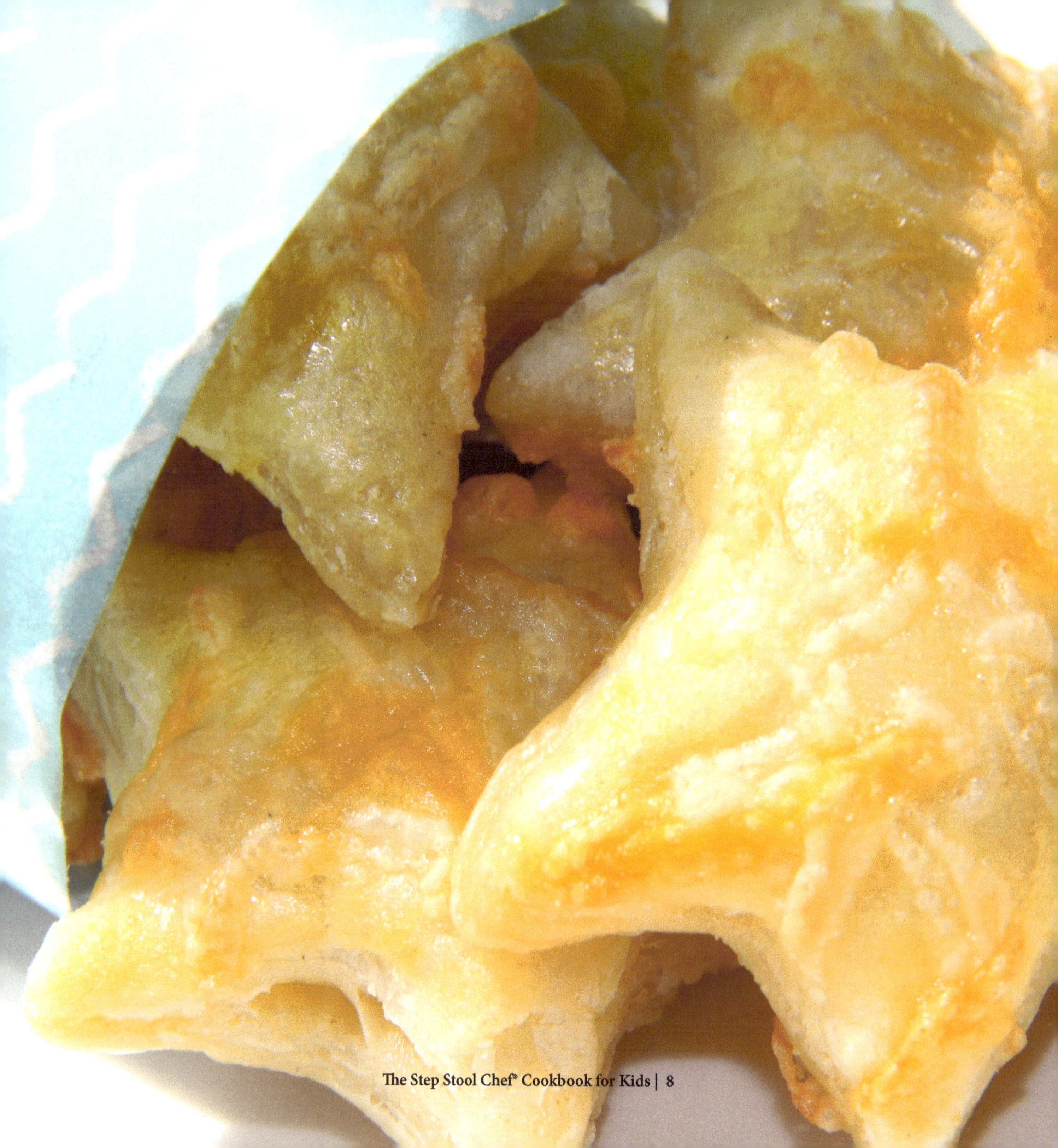

today's special

Easy Peesy Cheesy Puffs

INGREDIENTS

2 sheets of puff pastry
(found in the frozen section)
1 egg
1 tablespoon water
1/4 cup cheese, grated

INSTRUCTIONS

1. Preheat the oven to 350 degrees and thaw out pastry dough according to the instructions on the box.
2. Mix egg and water to create egg wash.
3. Cut shapes from puff pastry using a cookie cutter
4. Lay shapes onto a sheet of parchment paper on your baking pan and brush with egg wash.
5. Sprinkle a little cheese onto each shape.
6. Bake for 10 minutes or until cheese has melted and pastry puffed.

Step-by-Step Recipe on page 26

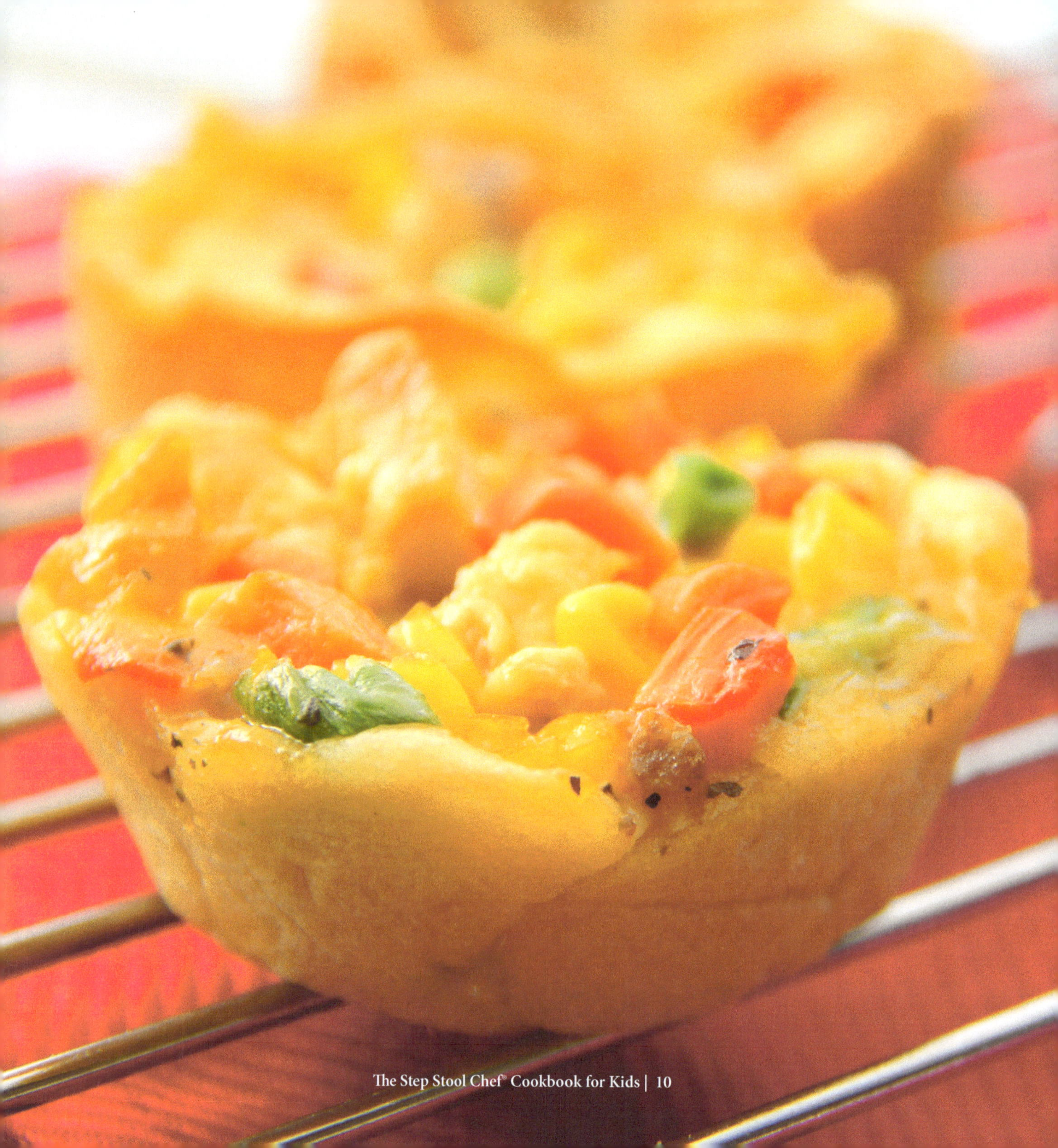

today's special

Mini-Muffin Chicken Pot Pie

Step-by-Step Recipe on page 27

INGREDIENTS

1 can or batch of crescent dough
10.75 oz of cream of chicken soup
1 cup of mixed vegetables
1 cup of cubed chicken
salt and pepper to taste

INSTRUCTIONS

1. Preheat the oven to 375 degrees. Lay your crescent dough flat then use a 3-inch cookie cutter to make round shapes.
2. Lay the round dough shapes in the muffin pan and press along the bottom & sides.
3. Mix cream of chicken soup with 1 cup of cubed chicken and 1 cup of mixed vegetables in a bowl. Add salt and pepper to taste.
4. Spoon the filling mix into the cups with about 1-2 tablespoons per cup.
5. Bake for 15 minutes or until golden brown. Let cool on cookie sheet for 3-5 minutes.

The Step Stool Chef® Cookbook for Kids | 12

today's special

Pizza Burgers

Step-by-Step Recipe on page 28

INGREDIENTS

PIZZA SAUCE
1 tomato, diced
6oz of tomato paste
½ teaspoon dried Italian herb seasoning
½ teaspoon sugar
¼ teaspoon salt
⅛ teaspoon black pepper

BURGERS
1 lb ground turkey
1 teaspoon steak seasoning
1 teaspoon onion powder
1 tablespoon Worcestershire sauce
1 tablespoon dried Italian herb seasoning
2 slices of mozzarella cheese
8 whole wheat hamburger slider buns
1 tablespoon chopped fresh parsley (for garnish)
 salt & pepper to taste

INSTRUCTIONS

1. For the Pizza Sauce, dice the tomato by hand or with a food processor. Add the diced tomatoes, tomato paste, Italian herb seasoning, salt, and black pepper, and cook until thickened, about 5 minutes, stirring frequently. Set aside.
2. For the Burgers, use your hands to mix the ground turkey steak seasoning, Worcestershire sauce, onion powder, Italian herb seasoning, salt & pepper in a large bowl; be careful not to over-mix the meat. Shape the meat into 8 small balls.
3. Grill the burgers over medium-high heat until done (hamburger meat should be cooked until it's no longer pink in the center) for about 6-8 minutes.
4. While burgers are cooking, divide each slice of mozzarella cheese into 4 smaller slices.
5. Place the burgers on the bottom bun on a baking pan then top with spoonful of sauce and small slice of cheese. Broil on low heat for 5 minutes until the cheese melts.
6. Sprinkle the parsley on top of the cheese and add the top bun. Serve and enjoy!

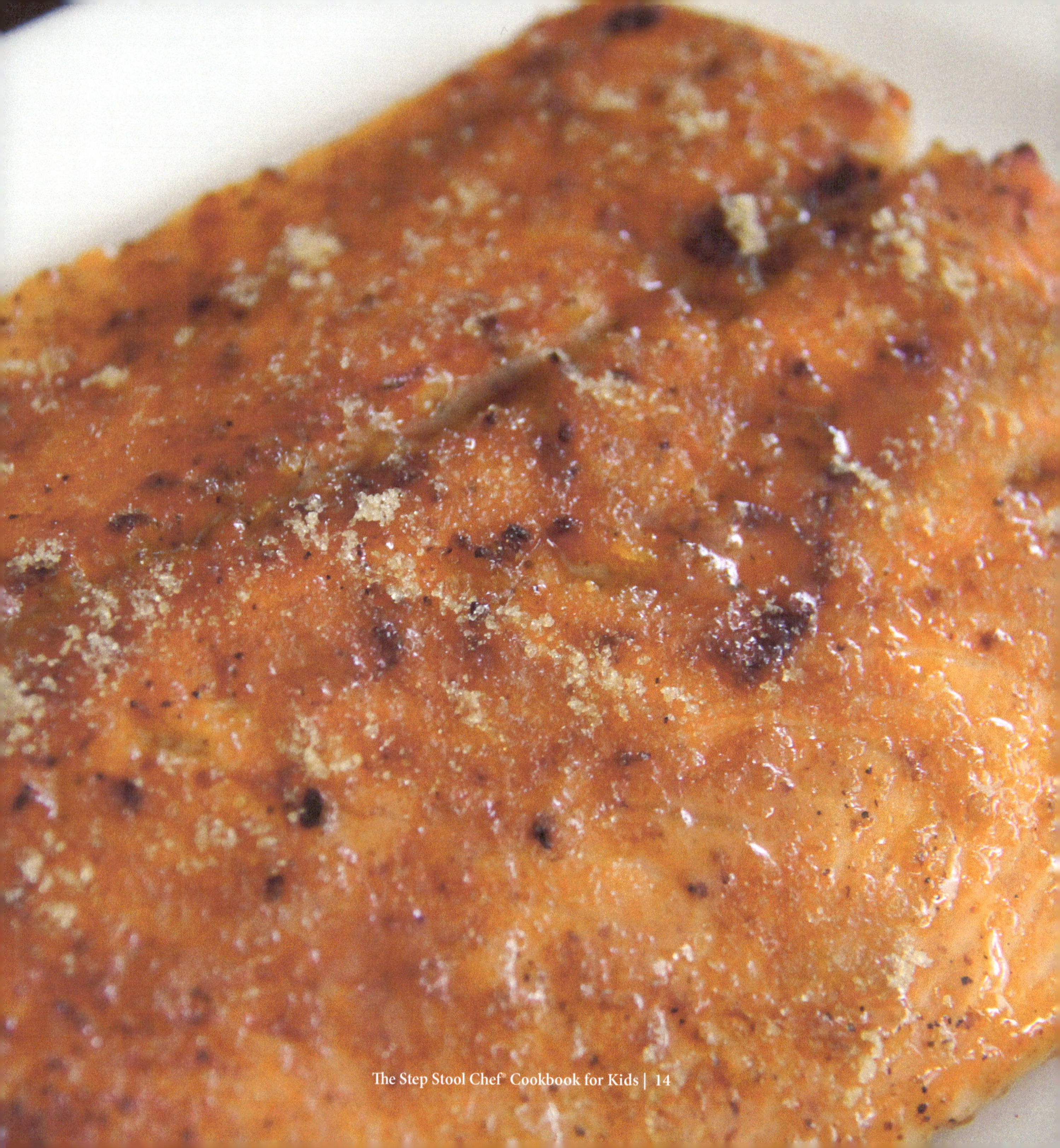

Salmon with Brown Sugar Glaze

today's special

INGREDIENTS

1/4 cup brown sugar
2 tablespoons honey dijon mustard

1 large boneless salmon fillet
salt & pepper to taste

Step-by-Step Recipe on page 29

INSTRUCTIONS

1. Preheat the oven to 400 degrees.
2. Place salmon in baking dish & season both sides of the salmon with salt & pepper.
3. Add the honey dijon mustard and brown sugar to a bowl.
4. Whisk together the ingredients.
5. Spoon a generous amount of the glaze mixture evenly on top of salmon fillets.
6. Place salmon in preheated oven for 20 minutes.
7. Then turn on broiler for 5-10 minutes or until the salmon is golden brown to desired level.

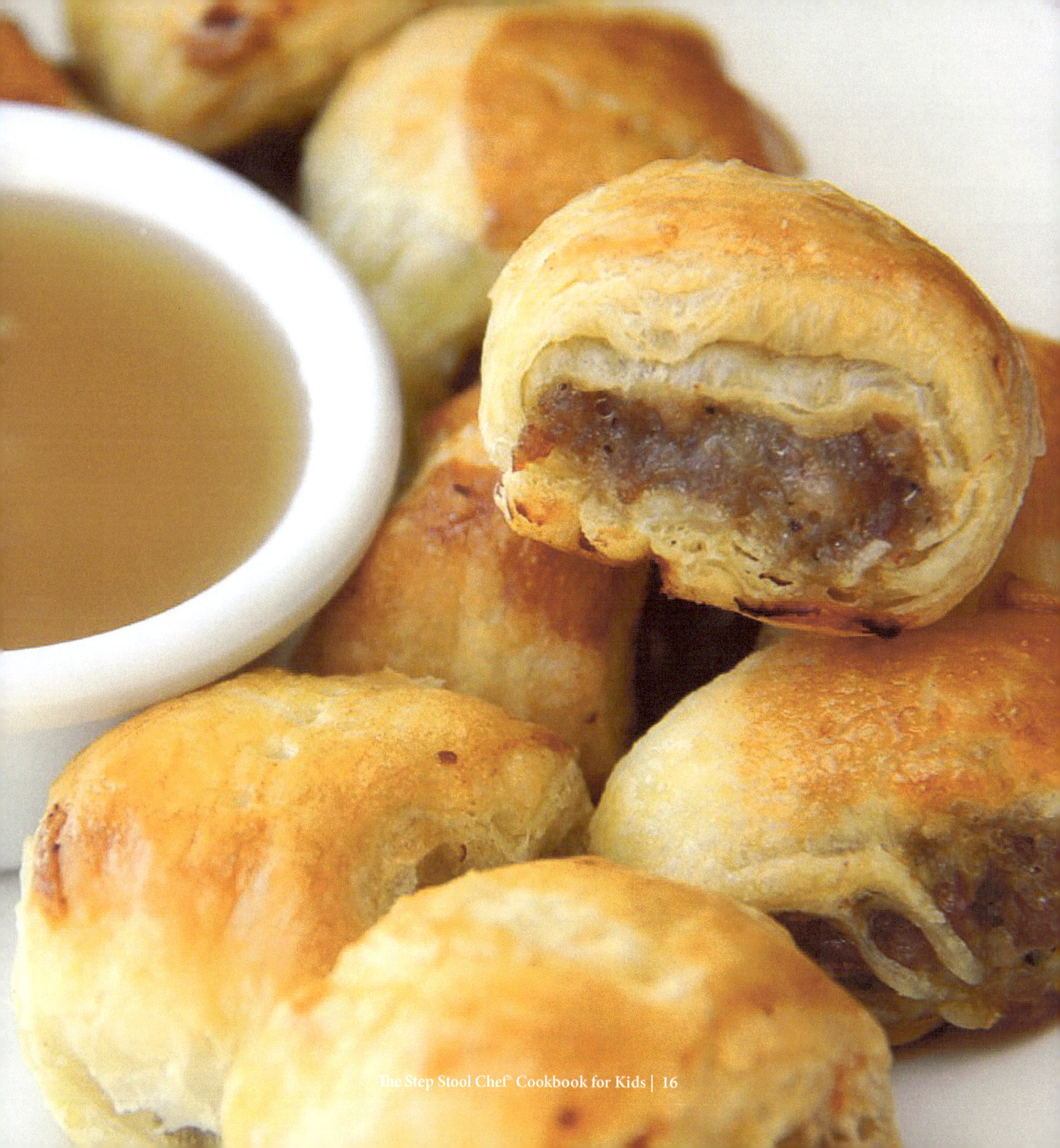

Sausage Bites
with Lemon Maple Sauce

today's special

Step-by-Step Recipe on page 30

INGREDIENTS

FOR SAUSAGE BITES
1 12 oz. package of breakfast sausage patties
2 puff pastry sheets (found in frozen section)
1 egg
1/4 cup bread crumbs
1/4 cups of parsley, cut
1 teaspoon thyme
1 teaspoon salt
1 teaspoon pepper

FOR EGG WASH
1 egg
1 tablespoon water

FOR MAPLE LEMON SAUCE
1/2 cup maple syrup
1/2 lemon, juiced
1/2 cup honey
1/2 cup water
1 tablespoon cornstarch

INSTRUCTIONS

FOR SAUSAGE BITES

1. Preheat oven to 425 degrees. Unwrap puff pastry sheets and lay on parchment paper then set aside.
2. In a mixing bowl, mix the sausage, breadcrumbs, eggs, thyme, parsley, and salt & pepper with your hands.
3. Cut along the pastry puff sheets fold lines to create three strips.
4. Take a small amount of the sausage mix and place down the center of puff pastry strips.
5. Fold the long sides of puff pastry over to meet in middle and press seam to seal.
6. Cut each roll into small equal pieces (about 2 inches).
7. Make an egg wash by beat 1 egg and 1 teaspoon of water. Place on baking sheet and brush the rolls with egg wash.
8. Poke holes in the middle of the small rolls to prevent over puffing.
9. Bake for 15 to 20 minutes, until puffed and golden brown.
10. Follow the same steps with the remaining sausage and puff pastry.

FOR MAPLE LEMON SAUCE

1. Over medium-high heat, combine honey, lemon juice and maple syrup in a saucepan.
2. Combine water and cornstarch and stir in water mixture.
3. Cook and stir until mixture thickens.

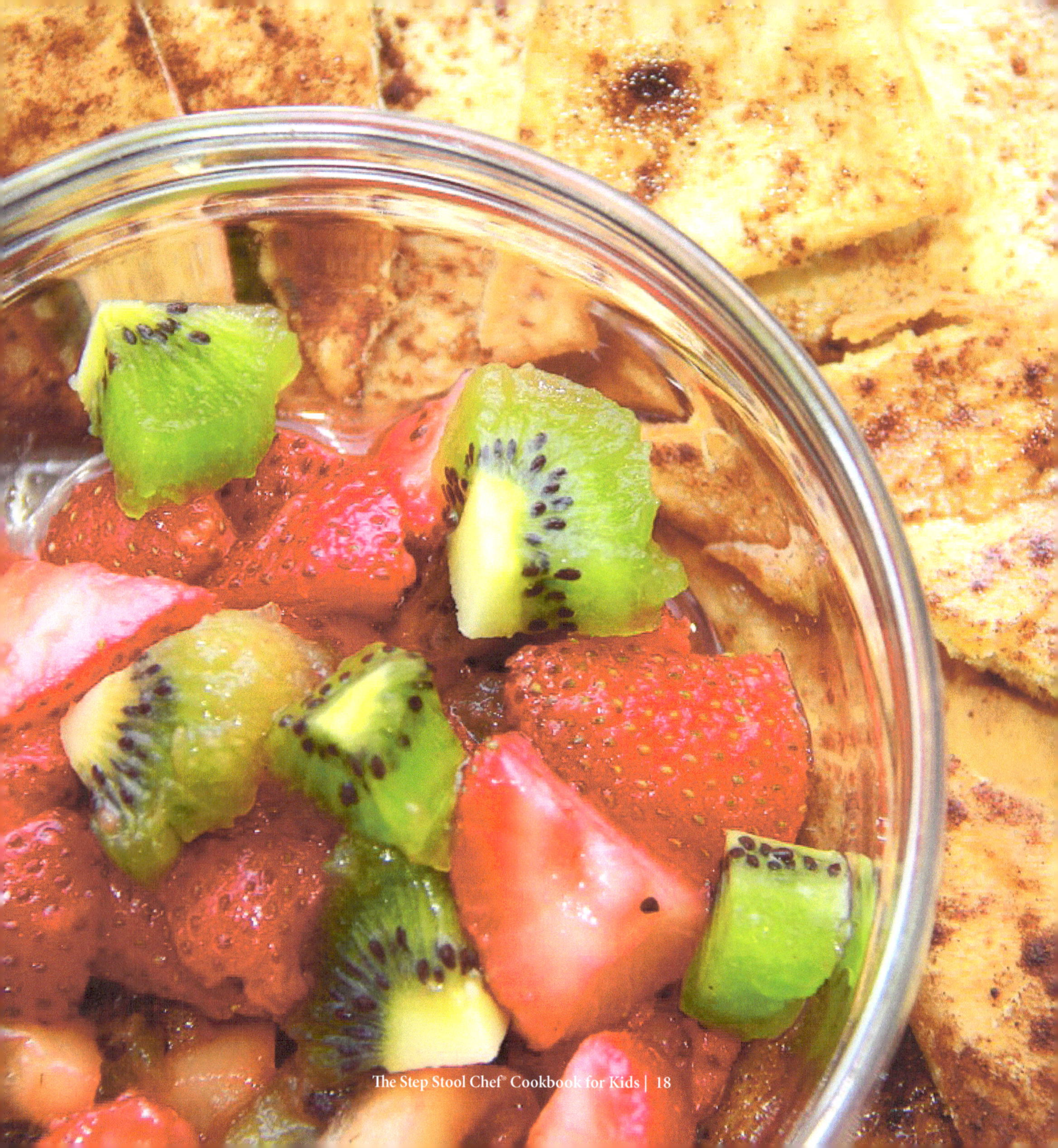

today's special

Strawberry Salsa
with Cinnamon Pita Chips

INGREDIENTS

STRAWBERRY SALSA

1 lb fresh strawberries, chopped
2 whole kiwi, peeled and chopped
½ a lime, juiced

CINNAMON PITA CHIPS

2 whole pita bread rounds
1 tablespoon of coconut oil
ground cinnamon to taste

INSTRUCTIONS

1. Preheat the oven to 350 degrees F.
2. Wash and chop the fruit for the salsa, mix together in a bowl, add the lime juice and set aside.
3. Cut the pita bread into 8 triangles using a pizza cutter.
4. Brush coconut oil and sprinkle with cinnamon on both sides of the pita triangles.
5. Arrange the triangles in a single layer on a cooking rack or cookie sheet lined with foil.
6. Bake in the preheated oven for 5-7 minutes. If you place them on a cookie sheet, flip them over half way through. We used a rack and both sides got crispy enough without flipping.
7. Allow crisps to cool for 2 minutes. Serve and enjoy!

Step-by-Step Recipe on page 31

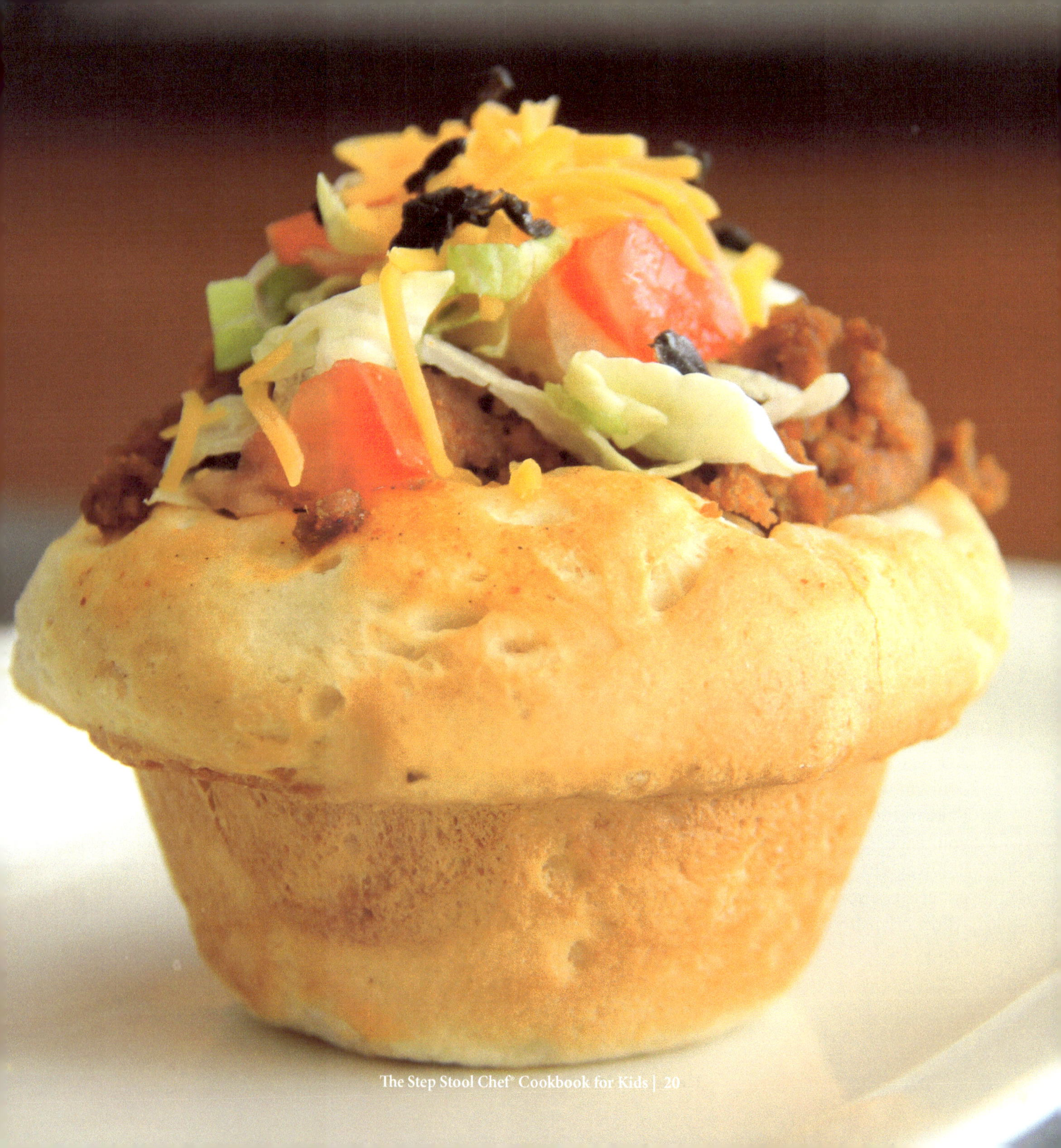

today's special

Taco Buddies

INGREDIENTS

1 pound of ground turkey
1 1/4 ounces of taco seasoning mix
1 can of buttermilk biscuit, refrigerated
1/4 cup of cheddar cheese, shredded

1/2 cup of lettuce, shredded
2 1/4 oz of black olives, sliced
1 large Roma tomato, diced
1 ounce of picante salsa

INSTRUCTIONS

1. Preheat oven to 400 degrees.
2. Brown ground turkey in skillet on medium high heat. Add the taco seasoning mix and water to the meat according to the package instructions.
3. Open the can of biscuits then separate and press one biscuit in each muffin cup. Shape the biscuit to the bottom and up the sides of each cup.
4. Fill each cup with seasoned cooked meat then place in the preheated oven and bake for 8-10 minutes.
5. While tacos are baking, dice the Roma tomato and put the remaining ingredients in separate bowls.
6. Remove the tacos from the oven and let cool for 5 minutes on cooling rack.
7. Add your toppings as desired and have fun decorating. Serve with picante sauce and enjoy.

Step-by-Step Recipe on page 32

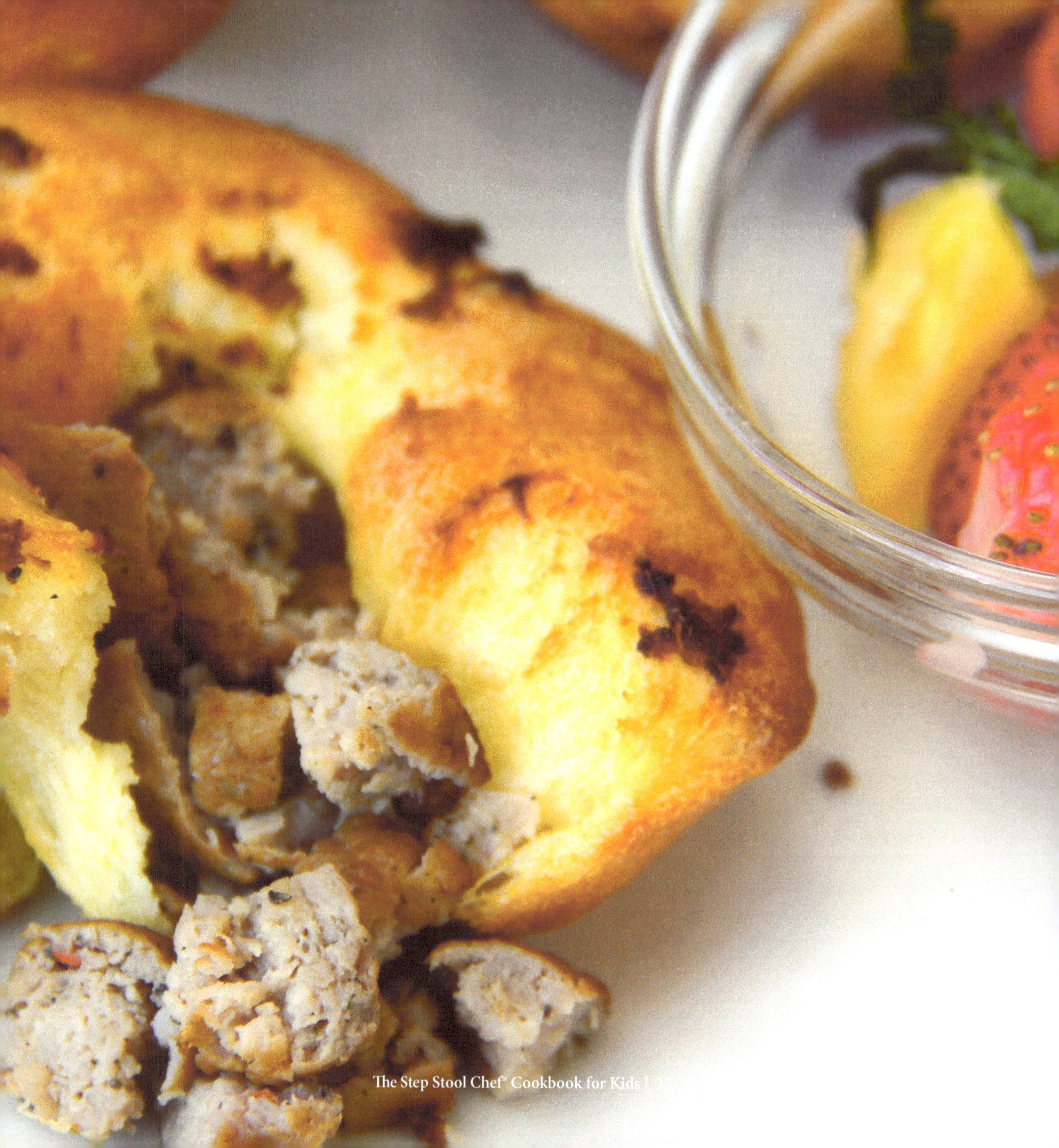

today's special

Turkey Sausage Popovers

INGREDIENTS

3-4 fully cooked breakfast turkey sausage links
2 eggs
1 cup milk

1 tablespoon olive oil
1 cup flour
1/4 teaspoon salt

Step-by-Step Recipe on page 33

INSTRUCTIONS

1. Preheat oven to 400 degrees and spray muffin pan with cooking spray.
2. Cut sausage links into small pieces and set aside.
3. In a bowl, mix eggs, milk, oil, four and salt until smooth.
4. Pour batter into the muffin pan and top with sausage then bake for 30-35 minutes until golden.

Baked Apple Bites
Step-by-Step Recipe

1. Preheat oven to 375 degrees. Peel apple then cut into 8 slices around the core. Using an apple slicer will make this easier.

2. In a separate small bowl, mix the brown sugar, cinnamon and nutmeg.

3. Unroll the crescent dough and separate into 8 triangles on a baking sheet lined with parchment paper.

4. Sprinkle sugar mixture evenly among triangles then place an apple slice at the wide end of the triangle.

5. Starting at the wide end of each triangle, roll the apple in the crescent dough. Brush the top with remaining tablespoon of melted butter then sprinkle the top with remaining sugar mixture.

6. Bake for 10-15 minutes then let cool for 5 minutes. Then enjoy!

Dutch Apple Crisp
Step-by-Step Recipe

1. Preheat oven to 375 degrees. Lightly grease ramekin cups or baking dish with cooking spray. Then begin to peel, core and dice apples in big chunks.

2. Place the apples in a large bowl. Then juice one lemon and pour juice in bowl of diced apples.

3. Mix honey, vanilla, cinnamon and nutmeg in bowl with apples.

4. Set aside the apples then prepare to make the topping. In a separate bowl add the oats, flour, cinnamon, brown sugar and butter.

5. Spoon the apples in a ramekin cup or baking dish then sprinkle over the apples.

6. Bake in the oven at 375 degrees at 30-40 minutes. Let cool and enjoy!

Easy Peesy Cheesy Puffs
Step-by-Step Recipe

1. Preheat the oven to 350 degrees and thaw out pastry dough according to the instructions on the box. Mix egg and water to create egg wash.

2. Cut shapes from puff pastry using a cookie cutter.

3. Lay shapes onto a sheet of parchment paper on your baking pan.

4. While on the baking sheet brush the shapes with egg wash.

5. Sprinkle a little cheese onto each shape.

6. Bake for 10 minutes or until cheese has melted and pastry puffed.

Mini-Muffin Chicken Pot Pie
Step-by-Step Recipe

1. Preheat the oven to 375 degrees. Lay your crescent dough on a flat surface.

2. Use a 3-inch cookie cutter to make round shapes.

3. Lay the round dough shapes in the muffin pan and press along the bottom & sides.

4. Mix cream of chicken soup with 1 cup of cubed chicken and 1 cup of mixed vegetables in a bowl. Add salt and pepper to taste.

5. Spoon the filling mix into the cups with about 1-2 tablespoons per cup.

6. Bake for 15 minutes or until golden brown. Let cool on cookie sheet for 3-5 minutes. Enjoy!

Pizza Burgers
Step-by-Step Recipe

1. To make a homemade pizza sauce cut fresh tomatoes into chunks then place in food processor to create a chunky sauce.

2. Next, add tomato sauce, tomato paste and seasonings to a sauce pan and let simmer on medium heat. Cook for 5 min or until thickened.

3. Mix ground turkey, steak seasoning, Worcestershire sauce, and Italian herb seasoning in a large bowl. Use hands to mix (fun for kids)!

4. Roll meat mixture into a ball. We used an indoor electric grill to make it an easier experience. But cooking them in the oven is fine too. Cook for 3-4 min or until medium well.

5. Transfer the burgers on the bottom part of the mini whole wheat bun. Spoon the pizza sauce on top of the burger and add a small slice of mozzarella cheese.

6. Place the burgers with the sauce and cheese in the oven for about 5 minutes to allow the cheese to melt into the sauce. Place the top bun and enjoy!

Salmon
with Brown Sugar Glaze
Step-by-Step Recipe

1 Preheat the oven to 400 degrees Place salmon in baking dish or plate. Season both sides of the salmon with salt & pepper.

2 Add the honey dijon mustard and brown sugar to a bowl.

3 Whisk together the ingredients.

4 Spoon a generous amount of the glaze mixture evenly on top of salmon fillets.

5 Place salmon in preheated oven for 20 minutes. Then turn on broiler for 5-10 minutes or until the salmon is golden brown to desired level.

6 Remove from the oven, let cool for a few minutes and enjoy!

Sausage Bites
with Lemon Maple Sauce
Step-by-Step Recipe

1. Preheat oven to 425 degrees. In a mixing bowl, combine the sausage, breadcrumbs, eggs, thyme, parsley, salt & pepper and mix with your hands.

2. Place the unwraped puff pastry sheets on parchment paper and cut along the pastry puff sheets fold lines to create three strips.

3. Take a small amount of the sausage mix and place down the center of puff pastry strips. Fold the long sides of puff pastry over to meet in middle and press seam to seal.

4. Cut each roll into small equal pieces (about 2 inches). Make an egg wash by beat 1 egg and 1 teaspoon of water. Place on baking sheet and brush the rolls with egg wash.

5. With a fork, poke holes in the middle of the small rolls to prevent over puffing. Bake for 15 to 20 minutes, until puffed and golden brown.

6. For the sauce, combine honey, lemon juice and maple syrup in a saucepan over medium heat. Combine water and cornstarch and stir in water mixture. Cook and stir until mixture thickens.

Strawberry Salsa
with Cinnamon Pita Chips
Step-by-Step Recipe

1 Preheat oven to 350 degrees. Wash and chop the fruit for the salsa, mix it together in a bowl, and add the lime juice. Cover the bowl and set aside.

2 Cut the pita bread into 8 triangles. Place wax or parchment paper underneath for easy cleanup.

3 Brush coconut oil on both sides of the pita triangles.

4 Sprinkle pita triangles with cinnamon on both sides.

5 Arrange the triangles in a single layer on a cooking rack or cookie sheet lined with foil.

6 Bake for 5-7 minutes. Allow crisps to cool for 2 minutes. Serve and enjoy!

Taco Buddies
Step-by-Step Recipe

1. Preheat oven to 400 degrees. Brown ground turkey in skillet on medium high heat. Add the taco seasoning mix.

2. Separate and press one biscuit in each muffin cup. Shape the biscuit to the bottom and up the sides of each cup.

3. Fill each cup with cooked meat then place in the preheated oven and bake for 8-10 minutes.

4. Remove the tacos from the oven and let cool for 5 minutes on cooling rack.

5. Add your toppings as desired and have fun decorating.

6. Serve with picante sauce and enjoy.

Turkey Sausage Popovers
Step-by-Step Recipe

1 Preheat oven to 400 degrees and spray muffin pan with cooking spray. Cut sausage links into small pieces and set aside.

2 In a bowl, mix eggs, milk, oil, four and salt until smooth.

3 Pour batter into the muffin pan until more than 1/2 full.

4 Add the cut sausage on top of the batter. Set aside any leftovers. We will use it later.

5 Place the muffin pan in a preheated oven and bake for 30-35 minutes until golden and poofy.

6 Warm the remaining sausage in a microwave or stovetop and add to the center of the Popover. Serve with fruit, preserves, honey or syrup.

the StepStoolChef®

Join in on the Fun!

Take a picture of your little Step Stool Chef® being a **Leader in the Kitchen** and share it with us.

Send an email to
thechef@stepstoolchef.com
or post on social media
using the hashtag #stepstoolchef

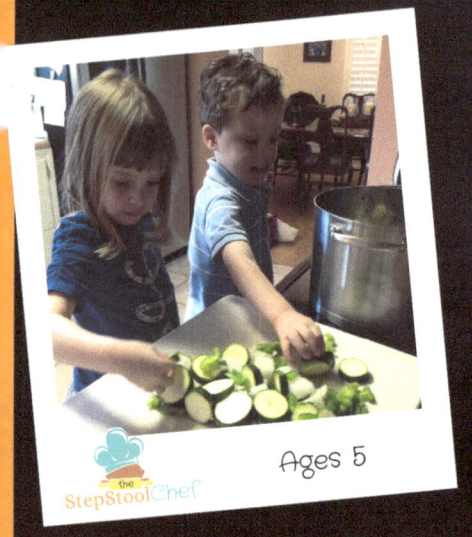

Ages 5

Age 6

Age 11